Sleepover Party

Sleepover Party

Cool Ideas For The Best Slumber Party Ever!

Susie Johns

4

About the author
Susie Johns is an artist, writer, and teacher who specializes in creative projects for children and young people. The designer behind all the models and art projects for *"Art Attack"* magazine, she also contributes to numerous other magazines, writing and illustrating features on creative crafts. Susie has written a number of art and craft books on subjects such as painting, drawing, photography, papier mâché, glass painting, collage, and embroidery. She lives in London, England, with her three children.

This is a Parragon Publishing Book

First published in 2004

Parragon Publishing
Queen Street House
4 Queen Street
Bath BA1 1HE, UK

Copyright © Parragon 2003

Designed, produced, and packaged by
Stonecastle Graphics Limited

Text, projects, and food by Susie Johns
Illustrations by Nicholas Owen
Edited by Gillian Haslam
Designed by Sue Pressley and Paul Turner
Photography by Roddy Paine

ISBN 1-40542-951-8

Printed in China

Disclaimer
This book is fun and will provide many hours of inspiration for children of all ages. Safety is very important. Young children should always be supervized by a responsible adult when participating in games and making the craft items and food and drinks described in this book. Care should be taken with scissors and other sharp objects and before commencing with any project you are advized to ensure the worksurface is protected. Always read the instructions supplied with paint, make-up, and face paints, etc., as they may differ from those given in this book. The publishers and their agents cannot accept liability for any loss, damage, or injury however caused.

Contents

About This Book
page 6

Party Planning
page 9

Food and Drinks
page 21

Party Girls
page 33

Games and Activities
page 45

Things to Trace
page 64

About this book

Whatever the occasion, your birthday, New Year's Eve, the end of term or the end of exams, it's a great excuse to invite a bunch of friends over and have a party. But there's one kind of party that's better than any other – a Sleepover! In fact, why wait for a special occasion? Why not have a sleepover next weekend – you know you want to!

This book is packed with ideas for things to make and do, from sending out your invitations to what to feed your friends before they go home, and masses of fun and games in between! There are beauty tips, dressing-up ideas, fortune-telling, recipes, and loads of fun activities.

With the help of this book you can be the hostess of the best sleepover party ever!

Party planning

You'll need to send out some invitations, decorate your room, and make some party plans. There's a whole section showing you how to do just that.

There's a checklist of what your friends should bring with them – such as party gear, chill-out clothes and, of course, their pajamas. And another list to help you make a timetable of events, such as games, activities, snack breaks, and bedtime.

And there are some great things to make, including decorations and name badges. Have fun!

Party food and drink

Your guests are going to be with you from dusk until dawn and beyond so you'll have to feed them! You don't have to be a celebrity chef to conjure up some tasty morsels to tickle their taste buds.

Just turn to page 21 for some ravishing recipes, from fun, fruity party cocktails to dips, pizzas, bedtime drinks and cookies, and some brilliant breakfast trays! Follow the simple recipes and your sleepover guests will certainly not go hungry!

Games to play

It's not a proper party without some fun and games! OK, if you're stuck for entertainment, you can always watch a video – but why not be more imaginative?

You could dress up as movie stars and act out your own Hollywood blockbuster! Or turn out the lights and scare each other with spooky stories! Or what about trying to tell each other's fortunes, or analyze each other's dreams?

This sleepover really is going to be the most memorable sleepover party ever!

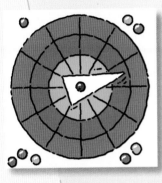

Be good!

Children may think that grown-ups have one main aim in life – to stop kids having fun! Actually, that's not true! But there are a few things you can do to make sure the party goes with a swing, without irritating the adults.

• Give them a copy of your party planner or timetable, so they know what to expect.
• Set some ground rules, such as which rooms you can use and which are out of bounds.
• Agree a mutually acceptable bedtime in advance – and stick to it!
• Don't make too much noise, and clear up any mess!
• Don't forget to thank the grown-ups for letting you have the party in the first place!

Party girls

Fancy experimenting with a new hairstyle, or messing around with make-up? With a bunch of girlfriends, what better excuse do you have to play at being hairdressers, or even give each other a complete makeover?

Turn to page 33 for hair-styling ideas, fantasy face painting, novelty nails, and useful beauty tips. Why not turn your bedroom into a beauty parlor for the evening?

A party to remember...

When the party is over and it's time for your guests to go home, make the event really memorable by giving each of them a special party bag with a few well-chosen gifts (page 18), or perhaps a decorated plate or cup as a personalized souvenir (page 16).

Make yourself a memory book, as a permanent reminder of all the fun you had (page 62). Then it's time to wave your guests goodbye... and start planning your next sensational sleepover!

Sleepover Album

Party Planning

You are invited...   10

Party bunting   12

Name badges   14

The personal touch   16

Bags of fun   18

You are invited...

Make your own party invitations – so much more stylish than buying them from a shop! With some scraps of colored paper, scissors and glue, just see what you can do!

Multi-colours

1 Cut a piece of cardboard measuring 9in x 7in. Fold it in half.

2 Cut out letters from colored paper to spell out the word "sleepover." You could cut individual letters from a magazine, or use a computer.

3 Stick each letter on to a scrap of colored paper and cut out a simple shape, such as an oval or a square or a triangle with rounded edges. Use scissors with wiggly blades, if you have them.

4 Stick the letters on to a different colored scrap of paper and cut out again. Also cut out some circles for a bit of added pattern.

5 Stick your customized letters on to the front of your invitation card. Now write your message inside – the date, time, and place of the party and a list of things your guests should bring with them.

Smiley faces

1 Cut a piece of colored cardboard 8½in x6in for each invitation. When folded this will fit into a standard size envelope.

2 Cut out circles of yellow paper. You could draw around a circular object such as a glass or a roll of sticky tape.

3 With a black felt-tip pen, draw a smiley face on each circle. These do not have to be exactly the same – vary them, if you like, with lop-sided smiles!

4 Stick a smiley face on the front of each folded card, then write your message below. You will find some fancy lettering to copy on page 64

What to bring

Here's a useful checklist of items your guests may need to pack in their overnight bag...

Party gear
A sparkly top and pants or skirt, or a disco diva dress, to get into the party mood!

Chill-out clothes
Tracksuit pants and a T-shirt, to slouch on the couch!

Pajamas or nightie
For bedtime – whenever that may be!

Brush and comb
Handy for hairstyling or simply brushing out the tangles!

Soap and wash cloth
To freshen up!

A favorite cuddly toy
Every girl should have one!

Sleeping bag or duvet
If you're sleeping on the floor, it'll be a lot comfier to have a cozy sleeping bag to snuggle into or a downy duvet to wrap up in! Add a plump pillow or some cushions to rest sleepy heads on!

...and don't forget your toothbrush!

Party planner

Write yourself a checklist before the party. This could include games and activities, snack breaks, TV or video viewing times, bedtime and pick-up time the next morning. Use this book to help you make your own personal plan. Here is an example...

4.30 pm	Put up decorations and hang sign on door
5.00 pm	Guests arrive – take bags up to bedroom
5.15 pm	Make name badges
5.45 pm	Cocktails, dips, and a chat
6.15 pm	Hair, nails, and make-up
7.00 pm	Fortune-telling and horoscopes
7.45 pm	Dress up
8.00 pm	Pizzas
8.30 pm	Video show
10.00 pm	Change into pajamas
10.15 pm	Bedtime drink
10.30 pm	Bedtime (yeah, right!)
10.45 pm	Spooky stories
8.30 pm	Wake up and analyze dreams!
9.00 am	Breakfast
9.45 am	Get dressed (casual!)
10.00 am	Video
12.00 noon	Pick-up

Party bunting

To put everyone in party mood, you may want to jazz up your room a little! It's amazing what a fantastic effect a few festive flags can have!

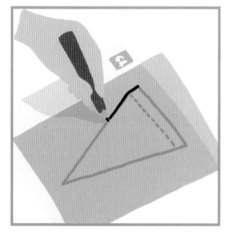

1 Trace the flag template from page 64, stick it on to a piece of cardboard, and cut out.

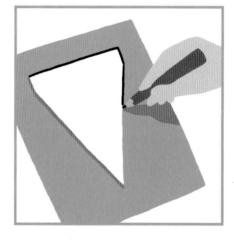

2 Draw around your flag template on to colored paper.

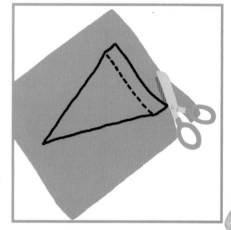

3 Cut out the flag shapes.

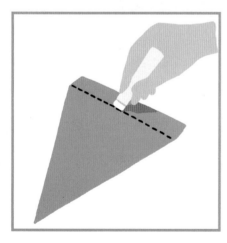

4 Apply glue to the top edge of each flag.

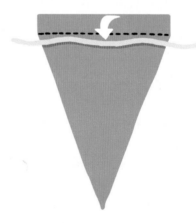

5 Place the string across the flag, about 3/4in from the top edge, fold over, and stick in place.

6 Space flags about 2in apart. Make sure you leave plenty of string at each end, so you can hang up your bunting!

Color schemes

Bunting is traditionally made up of flags of different colors for a bright, multicolored effect. You can use your own combinations of colors – it may depend on what colored paper you have available. Or why not make flags from a single color – you could even co-ordinate these with your invitations, party bags etc. And why not add some smiley faces?

You could make the decorations before your guests arrive – but it's much more fun to get your friends involved!

Name badges

OK, so you probably know each other's names already – but you could always be someone else for the night! These badges are really groovy! So get the girls together and have fun cutting, sticking, and pinning!

Before you begin

Get together some scraps of cardboard and paper, felt tip pens, scissors, stickers, glue stick, and safety pins, plus some strong sticky tape – electrical tape is ideal.

Want to be a star for the evening? Forget your own name and try on someone else's for size!

Choose your favorite pop singer, movie star, model, fictional character – anyone you wanna be!

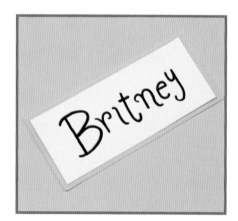

1 Write your chosen name on a scrap of paper. There's some fancy lettering on page 64, for you to copy if you wish.

2 Trim the paper to a neat rectangle, with scissors.

3 Stick the paper name label on to a second scrap of paper and trim, leaving a narrow margin.

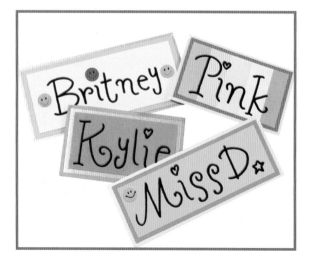

4 Now stick it on to a piece of cardboard and trim again to create a bright multicolored border. Finish off your design with stars, hearts, and stickers.

5 Attach a safety pin to the reverse of the badge, with a small piece of sticky tape.

While you've got your scissors out, why not cut out some funky patterns and make these into badges, too? For the simplest design, cut out circles of different sizes and stick them on top of one another. Or cut out flower shapes. Stick them on to a piece of cardboard and add a pin to the back, as before.

Door sign

Make this bright and bold!

Start with a large rectangle of colored cardboard. You could use the side of a cardboard box, covered with colored paper.

1 Cut out letters from scraps of colored paper and stick these in place, using a glue stick. If you haven't got lots of colored paper, use a glossy magazine. You should find quite large areas of plain color on the photographs and illustrations.

2 Make two holes in the top of the sign, thread a length of cord or string through and hang on your door.

Double-sided sign

While you're being creative, why not make a second sign. Simply stick on cut-out paper letters on the reverse of the cardboard, to spell out your second message.

This sign says **"do not DISTURB"** *but you could choose one of the following messages or make up your own.*

Sleepover Zone

No Admittance – Party in Progress

Boyz Keep Out!

No Entry – Girls Having Fun!

Ssshhhhh! We Need Our Beauty Sleep!

The personal touch

Make your guests feel special with their own personalised mugs and plates!

Before you begin

Get together the following:
plain white china mugs and plates
porcelain paints
porcelain outliners
fine, soft paintbrush

Painted china

It is easy to paint designs on plain white china mugs and plates using special paints suitable for decorating china, but do seek a parent's permission first. Don't worry about spoiling the best dishes — the designs can be washed off after the party! But if you wish to keep your designs permanently, you can bake the china following the paint manufacturer's instructions. See the box opposite for hints and tips.

Rainbow plate

1 Using a fine, soft brush, paint simple stripes on the rim of a china plate. Use any combination of colors you like – porcelain paints, which can be bought from craft stores, are available in a wonderful selection of colors.

The best paints to choose for this project are opaque colors, as they will give a really bright result on white china.

2 If you do not intend to bake the china, paint only the rim of the plate to ensure the paint doesn't come into contact with the food. Leave the paints to dry thoroughly before using. The designs should take about 30 minutes to dry.

Flower mug

1 Paint a yellow circle for the flower center. Leave to dry for about 10 minutes, then add a squiggle of orange outliner.

2 Paint pink petals all round. Then paint individual leaves, using green paint, leave to dry for 10 minutes, then outline leaves using a green outliner.

Name plate

Use outliner paints to write a name on the rim of the plate, then add hearts, squiggles, and dots in other colors. Leave to dry before using the plate.

Personalised party gifts

For a special souvenir of the party, you could paint a plate or mug for each guest to keep. In this case, make sure the design is permanent. Leave your painted design to dry thoroughly and, following the manufacturer's instructions, bake the china in a hot oven to set the paint. It can then be washed in hot, soapy water without the design washing off – though it will not be dishwasher-proof!
Remember! Make sure you leave the paint to dry and harden for several days before baking – and always follow the manufacturer's instructions very carefully.

Hints and tips

• You will need only a few pots of porcelain paint, one or two outliners, and a fine, soft paintbrush.

• Choose water-based paints, as these are safe to use and can be mixed together to create a range of colors, and your paintbrush can be cleaned easily with soapy water.

• Porcelain paints are available in transparent, opaque, and frosted colors. The opaque ones produce the brightest results on white china – but it's up to you which ones you choose.

• With three pots of paint – red, blue, and yellow – you can mix shades of orange, purple and green. Or you may prefer to choose a funky combination of pink, lemon yellow, and lime green, or perhaps turquoise, purple, and orange. You decide!

• Outliners are tubes of paste-like paint with a thin nozzle which helps to create a fine line. Colored outliners are available in a range of transparent colors and create a slightly raised effect.

Bright idea!

Paper plates can be decorated easily with felt tip pens. Get all your friends to join in!

The simplest design is to draw stripes of color following the ridges on the rim of the plate.

Use non-toxic felt-tip pens and decorate the rim of the plate, not the area which comes into contact with the food.

Bags of fun

When it's time to say farewell to your friends, you may like to give them a little gift to say "thank you for coming."

Party bags are so much more personal if you customize them yourself. Just buy plain gift bags and decorate them with your friends' names. Choose colors to match the party theme, if you like!

Cut out letters from colored paper and stick them in place using a glue stick.

If you prefer, you can buy sheets of peel-off and stick-on letters – the quick and easy option!

Party bags aren't just for little kids – it's what you put inside that makes all the difference! Here are some great ideas for cool contents!

- **Nail varnish** – the brighter the better!
- **Lip gloss** – look out for flower-shaped pots!
- **Stationery** – sharpeners and erasers are always useful!
- **Pens** – you can never have enough!
- **Key ring** – don't lose that locker key!
- **Hair brush** – colorful and crazy!
- **Chocolate and candy** – to satisfy a sweet tooth!
- **Scented soap** – to make bathtime fun!
- **Body glitter** – a party essential!

Buy plain gift bags and decorate them with stickers and transfers.

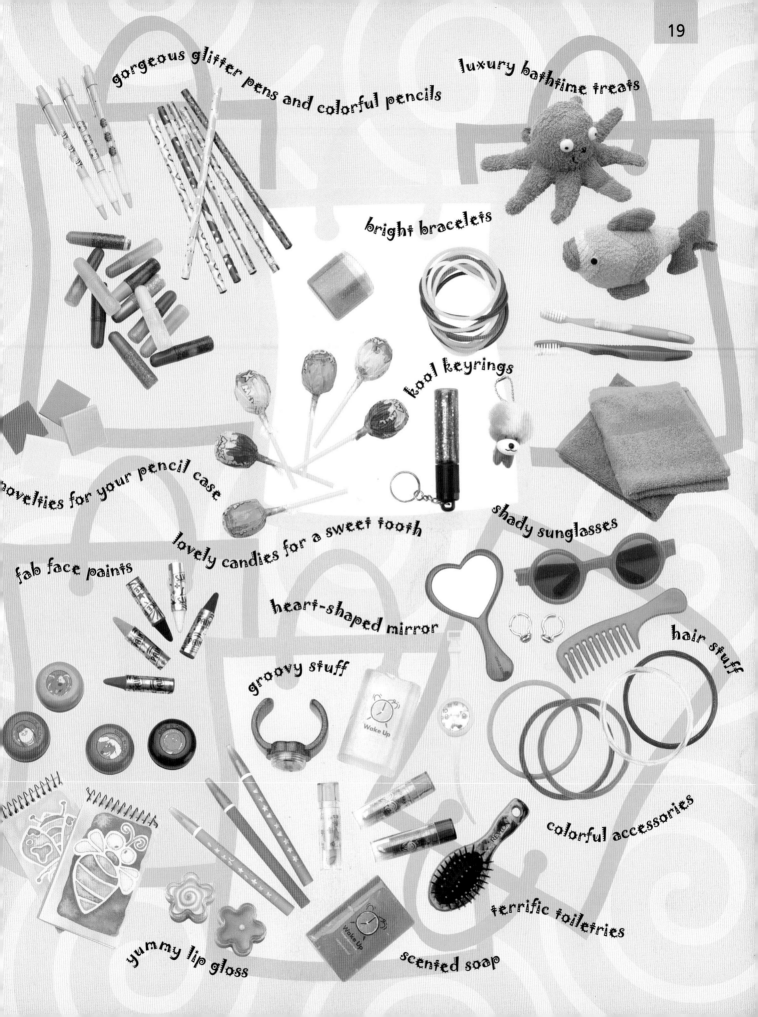

gorgeous glitter pens and colorful pencils

luxury bathtime treats

bright bracelets

kool keyrings

novelties for your pencil case

shady sunglasses

fab face paints

heart-shaped mirror

hair stuff

groovy stuff

lovely candies for a sweet tooth

colorful accessories

terrific toiletries

yummy lip gloss

scented soap

Food and Drinks

Cool cocktails   22

Dip'n'dunk   24

Pizza to go-go   26

Night cap   28

The brunch bunch   30

Cool cocktails

A great way to get the party started! These refreshing drinks not only look good, they taste sensational - and there's something to suit everyone!

Cocktail glasses

Decorated glasses make drinks more fun. Stores are full of funky tumblers – or you could decorate a plain glass using glass paints.

Surfer special

As blue as a tropical lagoon, to make this drink you will need a bottle of something blue and fizzy!

On the supermarket shelves, you'll may find several blue drinks to choose from, with fruity or even bubble gum flavors!

A squeeze of fresh lime will add a bit of zing and ensure the drink is not too sweet!

- Cut one or two slices from a fresh lime and reserve.
- Squeeze the juice from the remaining lime and pour into a glass.
- Top up with blue fizzy drink. Use the lime slices to decorate the glass and add a swizzle stick for stirring.

Down under

Kiwi fruit juice, available in cartons from most supermarkets, is a weird color and looks a bit like pond water – but it's deliciously fruity and refreshing!

Or use fresh kiwi fruits, mashed to a pulp or whizzed to a purée in a blender, then pushed through a strainer to get rid of the pips.

- Half fill a glass with kiwi fruit juice and add about a tablespoon of lime juice cordial.
- Top up with fizzy lemonade.
- Decorate the edge of the glass with a couple of kiwi slices.

Citrus sunset

This is not only very pretty to look at but, being made with orange juice, it's quite a healthy option!

Use carton orange juice or, for a really fruity flavor, squeeze juice from a few fresh oranges.

The "sunset" effect is fruit syrup – choose redcurrant, raspberry, or cherry.

 Pour orange juice into a glass until it's about three-quarters full.

Slowly and carefully, pour in fruit syrup. It will sink to the bottom of the glass.

Decorate with a slice of orange.

Sweet 'n' sour

Choose a red-colored fizzy drink for this great cocktail.

There are lots of different flavors available, most of them sickly sweet – but a dash of fresh lemon juice will help to balance that out, combined with cranberry juice from a carton for a double dose of Vitamin C!

Squeeze the juice from a fresh lemon (or use a generous amount of bottled lemon juice – about 2 tablespoons.

Pour it into a glass and top up with equal quantities of cranberry juice and fizzy drink.

Swizzle sticks and straws

Add a festive flourish to your drinks – transforming them into sophisticated cocktails – by adding a swizzle stick.

Not only decorative, they can be used to stir the drink and blend the flavors together. Mmmmmm!

Sipping the drink through a straw will make it last longer and taste even more delicious. Choose wiggly, curly straws for maximum fun!

Safer than glasses are plastic drinking cups – and they can be just as stylish! Even if you and your guests are careless and spill a drink (but please try not to!) there will be less chance of breakages if you use "safe" plastic tumblers!

Dip'n'dunk

You and your guests could get an attack of the munchies at any time – so be prepared for a snack attack! Whip up a dip to enjoy with potato chips or crunchy raw vegetable sticks. When it comes to crispy snacks you'll be spoilt for choice. Quick to prepare, these dips are not just fun to eat – they're healthy too! Remember to ask an adult to help you when you are preparing food in the kitchen.

Super Snacks

Bags of tortilla chips, with mild or spicy flavourings, tubes of wavy potato chips and bite-sized crunchy poppadums – provide your guests with a selection of these to dunk into your tasty home-made dips. And, as these packet snacks are very salty, include some crunchy raw vegetables, such as strips of red, yellow, and orange peppers or celery sticks, too, as a healthier alternative.

Sleepover Salsa

Make this as spicy or mild as you like. Basically, it has a refreshing tomato flavour, great with tortillas or any kind of savory potato snack – but you can add some Tabasco sauce if you want a bit of a kick!

Ingredients
3 tomatoes
1 scallion
2in piece of cucumber
3 tablespoons tomato relish
2 tablespoons tomato catsup
salt and pepper
Tabasco sauce (optional)

1 Chop up the tomatoes, scallion and cucumber as small as possible. Put them in a bowl.

2 Stir in the tomato relish and tomato catsup, then season with salt and pepper. Add a few drops of tabasco – but take care as it's very spicy!

Mexican Siesta

This is a variation of Mexican guacamole. "Siesta" is Spanish for sleep! Usually served with corn chips, or tortilla chips, it is just as delicious with sticks of raw vegetables. Once again, only add the Tabasco if you like things a bit spicy!

Ingredients
2 ripe avocados
1 tomato
2 scallions
1 lime
salt and pepper
Tabasco sauce (optional)
fresh cilantro leaves

1 Peel the avocados and remove the stones, then mash up the flesh in a bowl. Chop up the tomato and scallions as small as possible and stir into the avocado. Squeeze the juice from the lime and stir it in.

2 Season with salt and pepper and add a few drops of Tabasco, if you want. Chop up a small bunch of fresh cilantro leaves and stir in just before serving.

Say Cheese!

They say cheese gives you bad dreams – so don't eat this too close to bedtime! You can use Cheddar, Red Leicester, Double Gloucester – whatever cheese you have handy!

Ingredients
small carton of natural yoghurt
1/2 cup cream cheese
2 tablespoons mayonnaise
1 teaspoon French mustard
1/4 cup grated cheese
1 scallion, fresh chives or parsley (optional)
salt and pepper

1 Put the natural yoghurt, cream cheese, mayonnaise, and mustard in a bowl and whip up with a fork until well blended.

2 Chop the scallion, if using, or add some chopped fresh chives for a milder onion flavor. If you don't want a flavor of onion, add a generous handful of chopped fresh parsley instead. Season with salt and pepper.

Bombay dream

This dip has a mild curry flavour, great with mini poppadums!

Ingredients
small carton of natural yoghurt
4 tablespoons mayonnaise
1 teaspoon mild curry powder
1 tablespoon mango chutney
1 lemon
salt
fresh cilantro leaves

1 Put the yogurt and mayonnaise in a bowl and stir in the curry powder until thoroughly mixed. Stir in the mango chutney – use the sticky liquid from the jar, rather than large lumps of mango!

2 Cut the lemon in half and squeeze the juice from one half, stirring it into the dip. (Save the other half for another recipe, or to use in one of the cocktails on page 22.) Add a little salt, if you like, and garnish with a sprig of fresh cilantro before serving.

PIZZA TO GO-GO

Pizza is a popular choice – especially when everyone can add their own favorite combination of tasty toppings!

1 To make things easy, buy ready-made pizza bases, available from most supermarkets.

2 Allow one or two mini pizza bases per person and prepare a variety of toppings in advance.

3 Put each topping in a separate bowl for each person to help herself!

Have even more fun making funny faces with your pizzas!

Here is a list of toppings you may like to offer your guests...
- red onions, thinly sliced
- fresh chives, snipped into pieces
- canned sweetcorn, drained
- stuffed olives, whole or sliced
- sliced pepperoni sausage
- cooked ham, cut into strips
- grated cheese
- mozzarella cheese, sliced
- cherry tomatoes, halved
- red and yellow bell pepper, chopped
- canned tuna, drained and flaked
- canned pineapple, drained and chopped
- mushrooms, sliced
- fresh basil leaves
- chopped garlic

1 Spread each pizza base with tomato sauce. Use home-made sauce, or buy a jar of pasta or pizza sauce.

2 Add a sprinkling of grated cheese, which will not only taste good but will help to hold the other ingredients in place!

3 Then each add your own combination of toppings

HOW TO COOK YOUR PIZZAS

Pizzas need to be cooked for only 10 or 12 minutes – check the recommended cooking times on the packet!

For best results, place the pizzas directly on to the oven shelf, which will allow the heat to bake the bread bases, making them deliciously crispy!

Ask an adult to help take the cooked pizzas out of the oven using oven gloves.

Pizza tastes great cut into wedges and eaten with your fingers. Don't forget to provide lots of paper napkins for greasy hands!

Night cap

A hot milky drink will help you sleep – or so the grown-ups would like to think!

A mug of hot chocolate is a delicious treat – but give it the special party treatment and it becomes something really FAAAAA-NTASTIC!

1 For each person, you will need half a pint of milk and three tablespoons of drinking chocolate powder.

2 Check out your supermarket shelves for flavored chocolate drinks such as mint or orange, too. Some shops also sell flavored syrups, such as almond or vanilla, which are supposed to be added to coffee but taste just as delicious with hot chocolate!

3 Heat the milk gently in a pan on the stove over medium heat, or in a microwave. Take care not to overheat it or it will bubble over! Stir in the chocolate powder until it has dissolved.

Tip: whisking will make the chocolate deliciously frothy!

4 Pour the hot chocolate into mugs, then add one or more of these wicked toppings...

- EXTRA CHOCOLATE POWDER, sprinkled on top
- WHIPPED CREAM, squirted straight from the can
- CHOCOLATE SYRUP, drizzled from the bottle
- MARSHMALLOWS, floated on top or served on the side, for dunking
- CHOCOLATE FLAKES, whole or crumbled

There are all kinds of colorful decorations and easy-to-use icing tubes to choose from

Creative Cookies

Grown-ups are always saying, "Don't play with your food!" But sometimes rules like these are made to be broken. Here's a game that's fun to play, gives you an opportunity for artistic expression – and you can eat the results!

Choose plain cookies such as shortbread. They can be home-made or from a packet. Buy some tubes of ready-made frosting in various colors – some are flavored, too, with banana, strawberry, orange, and chocolate! Then put various toppings into small bowls and let everyone decorate to their heart's delight!

Biscuit Toppings

Check out the cake decorating section in your local supermarket, where you will find all kinds of colorful – or flavorful – edible decorations:

- MULTICOLORED SUGAR STRANDS
- SUGAR FLOWERS
- JELLY DIAMONDS
- CANDY BAUBLES
- CHOCOLATE FLAKES
- CANDY-COATED CHOCOLATE PIECES

THE BRUNCH BUNCH

AFTER a late night, it's good to start the day with a healthy breakfast. Here are some delicious ideas you may like to try. Ask an adult to help you when using the stove or the oven.

MENU 1
Orange Juice
Boiled Egg with Toast
Melon cup

MENU 2
Granola with Banana
Raspberry Smoothie

Orange juice

Melon cup

Boiled egg with toast

How to boil an egg

1 Pour enough water into a small saucepan to cover the egg. Place the pan on the stove, over medium-high heat and, just before it starts to boil, carefully place the egg in the water using a spoon. When the water starts to bubble, start timing!

2 For a large egg, cook for 4 minutes for a set white and a soft yolk. When the time is up, hold the pan under the cold faucet for about 8–10 seconds, then transfer the egg to an egg cup.

Melon cups

1 Cut a small melon in half. Remove the seeds and discard them, then scoop out the flesh.

2 Place the scooped out melon skins in small bowls. Chop up the melon flesh and add other fruits – whole grapes, orange segments, whole or halved strawberries, fresh or canned pineapple chunks, and sliced kiwi fruits.

3 Pile the fruits into the melon shells.

Granola

1 Into a medium-sized saucepan, put two cups of rolled oats, a tablespoon each of desiccated coconut, honey, golden syrup, and sunflower oil, and two tablespoons each of sugar and sunflower seeds. Heat gently for about 5 minutes, stirring occasionally, until the sugar has melted.

2 Spread the mixture on to a baking tray and bake in a medium oven (180°C/350°F) for 15 minutes, stirring halfway through.

3 Remove the tray from the oven and allow to cool completely, then break up any lumps by crumbling in your fingertips. At this stage, you can add other ingredients, such as chopped dried fruits – pineapple, papaya, and apricots, for example – golden raisins and toasted nuts.

4 Store the granola in a screw-top jar or plastic box for up to three weeks.

5 Serve a bowl of home-made Granola on its own or with milk, fruit juice, or yoghurt. Add slices of banana, too, if you like.

Raspberry smoothie

Granola

Raspberry smoothie

1 In a blender, put a banana, broken into chunks, and 3/4 cup of natural yoghurt. Pour in 2 cups of orange or pineapple juice. For a thicker smoothie, add a second banana.

2 Add a small can of raspberries, with their juice, and a few ice cubes. Whizz until smooth and pour into glasses.

This makes enough for up to six people.

Party Girls

Braids 'n' bunches   34

Pony tails   36

Novelty nails   38

Make over   40

Making faces   42

Braids 'n' bunches

Having a bad hair day? Or simply fancy a change? Whether your hair is long or short, straight or curly, there's a style for you! It's fun to play at being hairdressers! Why not take it in turns to do each other's hair and try some exciting new styles?

twist medium-short hair into small bunches

decorate each bunch with a tiny star clip

decorate long braids with lots of fancy hair accessories

use an elastic band to fix hair in a topknot

push chopsticks into the center of the top knot

a pair of braids keep long hair tidy

add a touch of sparkle with glittery scrunchies

Hair styling tips

Tying hair up with bands, or braiding, will be easier if the hair isn't too flyaway. Have a water spray handy, filled with warm water for damping down unruly hair.
Or try some different styling products:

• **MOUSSE** – will add volume to fine hair, or tame frizzy hair. Use a ping-pong ball size of mousse on slightly damp hair and work it into the roots of the hair, not the tips.

• **GEL** – available in different strengths, use this to sculpt hair. It's great for spiking short hair and molding fringes!

• **WAX OR SERUM** – will add shine and sleekness. Use it to calm down frizzy hair, to transform a wild, unruly mane into a headful of cool curls, or to mess up short, flat hair! Use only a tiny amount and rub between the palms of your hands before applying.

• **HAIRSPRAY** – is great for keeping styles in place but can make your hair a bit stiff! Try spraying a little on to your hairbrush to tame unmanageable hair!

How to do a hair wrap

1 Before you start, cut out a square of cardboard. Cut a slit from one side to the center, then make a small hole in the center, just big enough for several strands of hair.

2 Separate some strands of hair and slip the cardboard in place, positioning it at the hair roots. This helps to separate the strands of hair you are working on from the rest of the hair and prevents tangling!

3 Cut 4 lengths of embroidery floss, about 5 feet long and tie them around the hair, pushing the knot close to the roots and leaving equal lengths at both ends.

4 You will now have eight threads hanging down. Separate one from the bunch and hold the others, with the strands of hair, in your left hand (or your right hand, if you are left-handed). Start to wrap the single strand of thread around the bunch, round and round, quite tightly, for about 1in.

5 To change color, separate a different thread from the bunch you are holding, and add the thread you have just used to the bunch. Continue wrapping as before.

6 Keep changing colour like this. When you reach the ends of the strand of hair, you can stop, or carry on wrapping around the floss to make a longer wrap. Toward the end, instead of wrapping, you can braid the floss for a different look.

7 To finish, tie a knot to hold all the floss ends together, and trim off any untidy ends. Remove the cardboard.

Pony tails

You don't have to be an expert to create some really stylish hair effects – just a comb, some patience, and a few funky accessories.

You may think long hair is more versatile than short or medium-length hair when it comes to styling – but check out some of the groovy hair accessories and you may be surprised what you can do with your hair – or your friends' hair – whatever length it is!

Elastic bands

So practical – but they can also be fun! Great for tying long or medium-length hair in simple ponytails or bunches, they can also be used on shorter hair to create cute little topknots! Choose fabric bands which won't snag your hair.

Slides and clips

These come in all shapes and sizes and are practical as well as decorative. So useful for clipping back a fringe or holding stray strands of hair in place, they can also simply be placed anywhere on your head to add a bit of fun or sparkle.

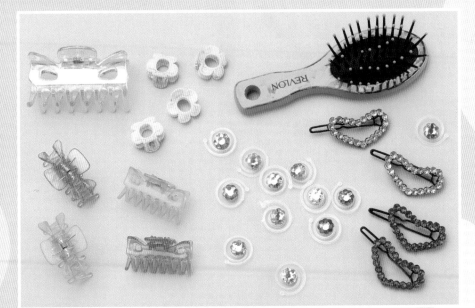

Ribbons

The classic adornment for hair, and really do add a lovely finishing touch. You can buy them in lots of different widths – narrow ones look great threaded into hair wraps and braids, while wider ones can be tied into bows or tied around your head to make a stylish hairband.

Scrunchies

Fabric strips with elastic inside, a quick and easy solution to keeping long hair tidy. They come in all colors and various different fabrics. Plain or fancy, if you've got long hair, they are indispensable!

Clamps and clasps

These are those things with teeth that spring open then clamp on to your hair. You can use the really big ones to secure a ponytail or medium and small ones all over your head to hold twists and braids in place.

Beads

Can be threaded on to the ends of hair wraps and thin braids and you can buy beaded hair accessories attached to coils of wire, specially designed to twist into your hair.

Alice bands and tiaras

Plain and simple or really glamorous! A fabric hair band is indispensable when it comes to keeping your hair off your face when cleansing or applying make-up, while fancier bands made from plastic or metal can really enhance a special party outfit.

Novelty nails

Ask your girlfriends to bring along some bottles of nail polish – chances are, they will have different colors from you so if you put them all together you'll have lots to choose from!

To apply nail polish perfectly, follow these simple steps:

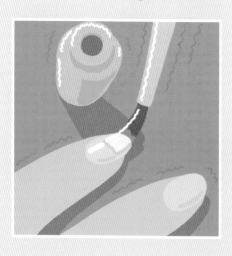

1 Rest the wrist of the hand you are painting on the edge of a table, to keep it steady.

2 Begin with a base coat, which helps to protect the surface of your nail. Starting with your little finger, paint a stripe of polish, in a single stroke, up the center of your nail from base to tip. Quickly follow this with two more stripes, on either side. Repeat with your other nails, then do the other hand. Leave to dry (about 2 minutes).

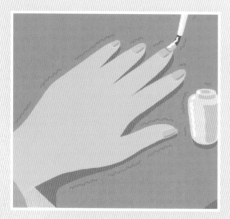

3 Now paint a coat of nail polish using the same method, described in step 2. Leave to dry thoroughly (about 5 minutes, depending on the nail polish used).

4 You may need to apply a second coat of color, or you may wish to apply a coat of clear nail polish which will give a lovely shiny finish and help to prevent the color chipping.

Colour choice

There are so many colours and finishes available, such a dazzling array, you'll be spoilt for choice!

There are glossy colours, shimmering colours, sparkling colours, polishes with glitter, sequins and holograms, and even scented polishes!

Do bear in mind, though, that unless you are very clever at applying nail polish, you'd be well advised to steer clear of very dark or bright colours which will show up any mistakes or smudges. Lighter colours are much more forgiving!

Also, as a general rule, reds look best on long nails, pale colours on short nails, pinks, greys and blues on pale skins and golds, oranges and yellows on dark or tanned skins.

Multicolors

Try combining different colors for a very groovy effect. If you have lots of different nail polishes, why not paint each nail a different color?

For vertical stripes, paint nails a single, pale color then, when this is dry, paint a stripe up the center of each nail using a different color. It is usually best to paint a dark color on top of a light one, as it will show up better.

For contrasting nail tips, you can paint the nail tip first with an opaque color and, when dry, paint the whole nail, including the tip, with a transparent color.

Or you can paint the whole nail first, with any color you like, then paint the tip with a contrasting color.

Once you've had a bit of practice, you will be able to paint all kinds of colorful designs – spots, stripes, flowers, it's up to you!

Nail decoration

You can buy special decorations to add dazzling designs to your painted nails – or you could use other stickers you may have, or even paper cut-outs.

• Some nail polishes already contain tiny sequins – but you can add your own sequins to plain polish.

• Or if you want a glittery effect and you don't have any sparkly nail polish, paint on a coat of colored polish, sprinkle your nails with glitter while they are still wet, then finish with a coat of clear polish to help to glue the glitter in place. Be sure to sprinkle the glitter over a sheet of paper and then carefully save it to use another day.

Beauty tips

Painted nails look glamorous – but chipped nail polish looks really tacky! So make sure you remove your artwork before it starts to chip. To do this, soak an absorbent cotton pad with nail polish remover and wipe it along the nail from the base to the tip. If you have applied several coats of polish, or if you have used glitter or sequins, it will be more difficult to remove, so try holding the absorbant cotton pad on your nail for a few seconds, to allow the remover to soak in.

an orange stick can be used to tidy cuticles

use an emery board to shape nails

spacers are used when applying polish to toenails

absorbent cotton can be used to remove old polish

Make over

Have fun with make-up – enhance your best features, add a bit of color and shine or go for all-out glitzy glamor for a special party. Here we show you how to achieve three different make-up effects.

a little mascara will make eyes look larger

Before the party, get together as much make-up and as many toiletries as possible. See if you can find a box to keep them in. And ask your party guests to bring things along, too. Here are some ideas for things to include in your make-up kit:

use a slick of lip gloss for lovely lips

- lipsticks, lip pencils, and lip gloss
- blusher
- eye shadows and eye pencils
- mascara
- face and body glitter
- stick-on jewels and sequins
- make-up brushes
- small sponges
- absorbent cotton pads and swabs

The natural look

You would think, to look natural, you'd need no make-up at all! But top models rely on a few tricks to enhance their best features. For a dewy skin, for example, smooth in some moisturizer. For a healthy glow, smudge a little cream blusher, or a spot of pink lipstick, on your cheekbones. And for lovely lips, rub in a little lip balm or Vaseline, or add a slick of lip gloss.

apply a little moisturizer to create a natural healthy look

make-up brushes are ideal to include in your make-up kit as they make it easier to apply blusher, eyeshadow, and lipstick

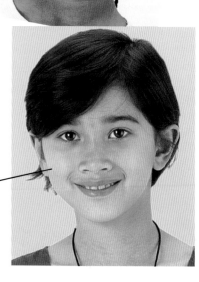

a touch of blusher will give you a beautiful glow

shades of pink and lilac look pretty

go for pink on eyes, lips, and cheeks

soft eyeshadow and peachy lips give a golden glow

Make-up for a special occasion

If you want to go a stage further, apply a little eyeshadow to your eyelids. If you are not confident, choose a neutral shade, or one that matches your eye color. Colored shadows are more difficult to get right but if you want to be more experimental, try plummy shades if you have green eyes, yellowy or coppery shades if you have blue eyes, and pinks or grays if you have brown or hazel eyes. Paint your lips with a colored lipstick – but not too bright.

green and gold on eyes and bronze shade on lips for subtle glamor

a bindi adds an exotic touch

use shades of gold for exotic eyes

use shades of pink for eyes – with a little glitter

Party glamor – go wild!

While you're messing about with make-up, why not go really wild? The grown-ups would never approve — but, so what? It's your party, you are in the privacy of your own room, and no one is going to see you, except your closest friends! Use every color available, plus a few stick-on jewels, to create madly exotic eyes, wonderfully glamorous lips, impossibly rosy cheeks, and as much sparkle and shine as you can manage! Wow!

use a little mascara for dramatic effect

stick on jewels add instant glamor for a special party

a touch of glitter looks fabulous

glitter eyeshadow pencils are great for a glamorous look

Making faces

Face paints aren't just for little kids — you can use them to create some stunning effects. By applying paint with a damp sponge, you can create subtle blends of color: try a rainbow, or a cloudy sky or a tropical sunset. Or use a fine, soft paintbrush to paint lines, dots, swirls, flowers, anything you like! Adding touches of glitter or stick-on jewels looks great too!

Using face paints
Only use paints specially made for face painting. Always follow the manufacturer's instructions. Do not use if you have an allergy which may affect your skin and never use face paint if you have a facial cut or sore. Keep your paints clean and wash out your brushes in warm soapy water.

EXOTIC Outline eyes with purple face paint, sweeping the lines up at the outer corners for an exotic effect. Paint arching lines above eyebrows, in red, then paint a motif of petals and curly lines on forehead, in pink. Why not stick on tiny jewels as a final flourish?

BUTTERFLY Paint the outline of a butterfly's wings, framing eyes, with purple face paint. Fill in the wing shapes with pink and blue, using a larger brush or a small sponge. Paint the butterfly's body along the center of the nose. Add stick-on jewels.

CARNIVAL MASK Use a damp sponge to apply white face paint in a mask shape, then dab pink face paint in the center and paint around eyes. Dab on small dots of smudgy blue and mauve diamonds.

DOLPHIN SPLASH Sponge on blue and yellow face paints to create sand and waves, blending colors together for a soft effect. With a paintbrush, add a blue dolphin and water splashes on forehead.

RAINBOW SKY With a damp sponge, cover face with a light coating of pale blue face paint and, when dry, dab on white clouds Then use a paintbrush to paint a rainbow arching over one eyebrow.

TROPICAL BEACH Use a sponge to dab on stripes of color across whole face, blending edges as you go, to create a sunset effect Then, with a paintbrush, paint a palm tree across one cheek and over eyes.

Face to Face

When it's time for bed, don't forget to clean off all your make-up!

So, you've had fun experimenting with hairstyles and creating fantastic faces – but you must clean it all off before you go to bed or you will end up with dirty skin and irritated eyes, not to mention smudges all over your pillowcase!

Soap and water – this is fine for removing most make-up, especially face paints. Use warm water and rinse your skin well to remove any traces of soap, then finish by splashing with a little cold water to refresh your skin and close the pores!

Cleansers – these break down the greasiest of make-up, including lipstick. Choose one that's suitable for both face and eyes. Follow the instructions on the bottle – some cleansers can be wiped off with absorbent cotton, while others are rinsed off with water.

Toners – these help to refresh the skin and close pores, which is thought to help prevent spots! Splashing cold water on your face has a similar effect. Or pour a little rose water on to absorbent cotton and wipe over your face.

Moisturizers – soften your skin by applying a little light moisturizer before you go to bed. You're never too young to start looking after your skin. Just use a little and smooth it all over your face with your fingertips.

Face pack – there are various kinds available, so check the label and choose the right one for your skin type. It will deep-clean your skin until it glows!

One more thing – don't forget to brush your teeth!

Games and Activities

Best of friends ... 46

Fun and games ... 48

Movie stars ... 50

Ghost stories ... 52

Fortune-telling ... 54

Horoscopes ... 56

Pajama-rama ... 58

Dream team ... 60

Keepsake book ... 62

Best of friends

Tying a thread around your friend's wrist will seal your friendship. It's said to question your friendship if you cut the bracelet off, but tie it loosely and you will be able to slip it off when you are at school. Otherwise, wear the bracelet until it falls apart and you will remain good friends!

Making a simple friendship bracelet

To make a friendship bracelet, you will need some colored threads. Embroidery threads, available from craft or notions stores, are ideal and they come in such an array of beautiful colors, you'll have difficulty choosing your favorites!

You probably already know how to make a simple three-stranded braid. Just in case you don't, here's how!

Take three threads of different colors, about three times the length you want your finished bracelet to be, knot one set of ends together. Knot the ends of the three threads together. Hold the three threads spread apart, bring the right-hand one between the other two, then the left hand one between the other two, and so on, right, left, right, left! When the braid is long enough, tie another knot, to stop your braid unraveling, and it's ready to wear. Just tie in place and trim off any excess threads.

Use the free ends to tie the bracelet around your friend's wrist – not too tightly! If you want to make a thicker braid, use six threads, or nine, or more (make sure the number is divisible by three).

Whether you choose to make a three-stranded or a four-stranded braid, you can have fun choosing your own favorite color combinations and be sure that you are making something that your friend will always treasure!

How to make a four-stranded braid...

This is slightly more difficult to do than a three-stranded braid but quite easy really, once you get the hang of it!

1 Cut four 32in lengths of embroidery floss.

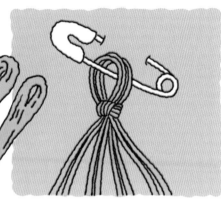

2 With all four threads together, fold in half and tie to make a loop. Use the safety pin to pin the loop to a firm surface – such as the leg of your pants!

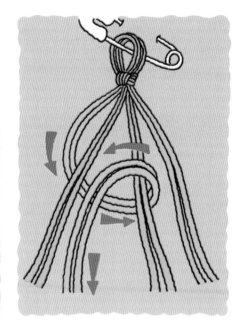

3 Hold one pair of double threads in each hand. Take one of the outside threads under the two middle threads and back over the thread it just passed under.

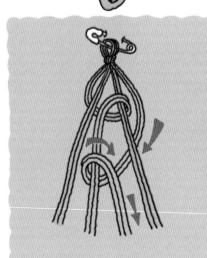

4 Then take the outside thread from the other hand and do the same, but in the opposite direction. You may find it easier to follow the diagram, right.

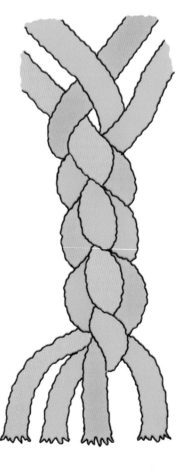

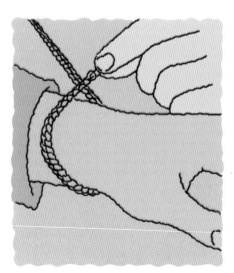

5 When the bracelet is long enough, tie a knot to prevent the threads unraveling, then tie it on to your friend's wrist and trim off the ends.

Fun and games

It's playtime! Here are some games that will not only be fun to play but could also – if you are lucky – help to satisfy any hunger pangs!

Dangling snacks

Use cookies or savory snacks that have holes in the middle – bagel chips, pretzels, and fancy iced cookie rings, for example! Or use mints with holes or other candies which can easily be tied in the middle with string such as soft twisty marshmallows or jellies.

Tie a number of these on to lengths of string and suspend from the top of a door frame, a curtain pole, or a washing line – check with a grown-up before doing this.

The aim of the game is to try to eat as many snacks as possible using only your mouth and with your hands well and truly behind your back – no cheating or you could be disqualified! Players are not allowed to eat the snacks whole and must take at least three bites. Take it in turns to be the referee who ensures fair play and who writes down the scores.

This is even more fun if the players are blindfolded!

Cornflake diving

Place several candies in a large dish, then fill the dish with cornflakes. Players take it in turns, with hands tied behind their backs, to retrieve one of the candies using only their teeth! Use a stop-watch to time each player – the fastest wins!

Chocolate challenge

Sit in a circle on the floor and, in the center, place a plate with a large bar of chocolate on it, a fork, spoon, hat, scarf, and a pair of gloves.

Players take it in turns to roll two dice. The first to throw a double six puts on the hat, scarf, and gloves, picks up the fork and spoon and uses them to try to cut off a chunk of chocolate and eat it. She can carry on eating the chocolate, using the fork and spoon – no fingers! – until someone else throws a double six, at which point they change places.

Keep playing until the chocolate has vanished!

Drinking race

Give each player a bowl and a plastic teaspoon. Fill each bowl with an equal amount of water. On the word "go" players have to drink the water using the spoons. The fastest wins!

Pass the cookie

If there are enough people at your sleepover, you could play this in teams!

Get into line.

The person at the front picks up a cookie from the edge of a table using her teeth. Her hands should be behind her back.

She passes the cookie to the person next to her – who takes it in her teeth, as her hands should also be behind her back. She then passes it to the next person, and so on.

If the cookie breaks, or is dropped, you have to start again!

You could play this game against the clock, to see how many cookies you can pass from one end of the line to the other, or to see which team is fastest and can pass the most cookies.

And you can bet that, not only will quite a few cookies get eaten during the course of the game – but there'll be a lot of crumbs to sweep up at the end!

PARENTS ARE ADVIZED TO SUPERVIZE EATING GAMES

Celebrity persona

Check out the name badge activity on page 14. Did you write your own name on your badge?

Why not write the name of your favorite pop star or actress instead. Or a character from fiction, perhaps? For the duration of the sleepover party, you can assume a different identity – you can reinvent yourself.

Who am I?

Here's another idea involving name badges, using names of famous celebrities or pop stars. Make a badge or a sticker for one of your friends. Don't let them see the name you have written.

Now pin it on the back of their shirt, where they can't see it. The idea of the game is to go round trying to guess what name you have been given, asking the other guests questions that can only be answered with "yes" or "no".

So you may ask, for example: "Am I a singer?" or "Am I a girl?" or "Have I got blonde hair?" until you have enough information to guess who you are! This game is good when played against the clock – simply decide on a length of time each player has to guess correctly – perhaps two minutes.

Movie stars

You're never too old to dress up! Ask a grown-up if you can borrow some glamorous stuff – a few sparkly tops or dresses, perhaps, or a fancy handbag and some high-heeled shoes. Or search your local thrift store or yard sale for some brilliant inexpensive items – a wrap or shawl, a few necklaces, or even a hat or some feathers!

Try to build up your own collection of gorgeous gear. Then, when the girls come round, you are ready to get dressed-up for any imaginary occasion – a pop party, a fabulous first night, a brilliant ball, or even the Oscars, darling!

If you can't find enough couture clothes, collect some pieces of frivolous fabrics. With some ribbons and safety pins, these can be draped and tied to create your own designer dresses! Add a feather boa and a sophisticated hairdo!

If the movies aren't your scene, why don't you and your friends dress as pop stars? You could even stage an audition or a singing competition, just like they do on TV!

"I'm ready for my close up!"

Dressing-up tips

- if your dress is too long, add a belt and pull up the fabric until it's the right length!
- make straps from lengths of ribbon pinned in place!
- make a long skirt into a dress – just pull it up under your armpits.
- if a hat is too big, tie a scarf around your head first, to pad it out a bit!
- if your tiara wobbles, use hair clips to hold it in place!
- scarves are versatile – use them as belts and sashes, to tie around hats, or wrapped around your body to make a top or skirt
- don't forget the finishing touches – a necklace, a feather boa, or some sparkly hair accessories

"Lights, camera – action!"

Now is the time to get out the camera and take some publicity pictures! Put on some music to get everyone in the mood, then strike a few glamorous poses!

Ghost stories

Turn out the lights and get out those torches – it's time to send shivers up your spines with some spooky stories!

 Make up your own tall tales. You could take it in turns to build up a story, bit by bit, from the first few lines to a shuddering climax. Someone starts the story, speaking for, say, two minutes before handing over to the next person to carry on with the tale for another two minutes, and so on. Each person should try to use her imagination, inventing creepy characters, petrifying plots and devilish dialogue.

Setting the scene

Before you turn out the lights, find some torch lights – and make sure they work (if not, try replacing the batteries!) Pile up plenty of cushions and wrap yourself in a blanket, duvet or dressing gown. Telling stories in a darkened room, with only torchlight to illuminate your faces will add to the creepy atmosphere – but in case anyone gets too spooked, make sure everyone knows where the light switch is!

Torch Tales

Here's a fun way to play! Have a single torch light and let the person who is holding it be the storyteller. She could tell a whole spooky story, or just a section, before passing on the torch light to the next person.

If you like, you could choose one of these starting points and let the stories develop into something truly terrifying...

It was a dark, dark night in Windy Hollow. Not a single star shone in the black sky. The wind whispered in the leaves of the trembling trees and small creatures rustled in the undergrowth. Suddenly, a blood-curdling scream pierced the chilly air...'

Mrs Brown was angry. This was their first vacation together in years and her husband had parked the caravan in the farthest corner of the remotest field, miles from civilization. "Don't worry," Mr Brown reassured his wife. "It's late now, and too dark and cold and wet to move. But first thing in the morning, we'll find a nice, busy, crowded caravan park. Now try to get some sleep." The clock chimed midnight. He turned off the lamp. Just moments later, there was a tap-tap-tap at the window...

Sarah hadn't wanted to move to the new house. She sat on the back step, keeping out of the way of the removal men, who were trying to unload the van before it got dark. Her mother called to her from the kitchen but she didn't want to go inside. She got up and made her way down the path, to the end of the garden, where it was overgrown with brambles and ivy and shaded by a big, ugly old tree. "Hello, Emma," said a voice which seemed to be coming from the bushes. "Hello, Emma, I've been waiting for you..."

It was the night of the school play and all the parents had taken their seats in the hall, waiting for the lights to go out and the curtain to go up. Backstage, everyone in class 6 was giggling with nerves. "All right, is everyone here?" asked their drama teacher. "No, Miss," said Alice, "Emma's not." "But she has the leading role," said the teacher, "wherever can she be?" "Well Miss," said Alex, "the last time I saw her she was heading towards the girls' washroom..."

The door creaked open and old Mr Jenkins appeared. Something furry brushed past his legs. "That'll be Tiddles, the cat," thought Mr Jenkins. But it wasn't Tiddles, it was...

Fortune-telling

Wouldn't it be fun if we could look into the future? Well, here are some ideas for making predictions: a spinning Wheel of Fortune and a special book that might just hold the answers!

You will need:
thick cardboard
pencil
ruler
glass-headed pin
bead
eraser
colored pencils or felt-tip pens

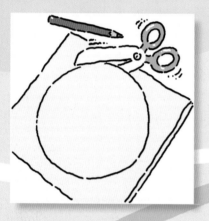

1 Draw a circle on a piece of cardboard and cut it out.

2 Divide the circle into twelve segments, then draw two smaller circles. You now have 36 areas in which to write predictions!

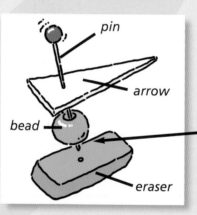

3 Colour each segment in one of three different colors.

4 Make a spinner by cutting an arrow from cardboard and pushing a pin through one end. Push the pin through a bead and then through the center of your colored circle. Finally push the sharp end of the pin into an eraser for safety and to protect your table.

pin

arrow

bead

eraser

colored circle is positioned between bead and eraser

5 Test the arrow, to see if it spins freely.

6 To play the game, take it in turns to pick a color (you could do this randomly, with colored buttons or counters), then spin the arrow and, when it stops, read the prediction on the appropriate section.

7 Before you spin, you could ask a question and see what kind of answer you get! For example, to the question, "Will I pass my music exam?" the reply might be "You have the potential." How you interpret this answer is up to you!

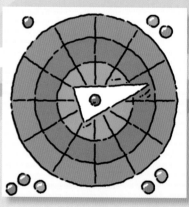

Book of Wisdom

Here's another idea! A Book of Wisdom. Simply start with a book that has blank pages. It can have as many pages as you like. The more pages, the more answers you will have to come up with because you need to write something on each page. You and your girlfriends can take turns in asking a question, then open the book at random to receive your reply. Once again, it's not just about the questions you ask – it's how you interpret the answer that matters! Add a title to the cover of the book. It could be *The Book of Answers, The Book of Fate,* or *The Book of Wisdom* – it's up to you... Good luck!

doesn't look good

absolutely

the future is misty

no

perfect match

ask again later

if you try

what do you think?

yes

don't even doubt it

maybe

there is hope

you bet

a match made in heaven

don't even think about it

it's up to you

Here are some suggested answers and predictions to put on your Wheel of Fortune or in the pages of your Book. Use your imagination to come up with some of your own, too...

You will achieve success
Change your goals
You will need assistance
Look to the future
Try a little harder
Happiness is on the horizon
You cannot do it alone
You will find inner strength
Beware of your enemies
Don't be afraid
Don't do it
Follow your heart
Respect your elders
A change is overdue
Good luck
You must choose
You are on the right path
You will find inspiration
You are incompatible
There are barriers
Think again
It's a dead end
Trust your instincts
You will fail
It's not important
Love will find a way
Pursue your wildest dreams
It was never meant to be
You are turning a corner
Lighten up
Start again
Carry on
It's trivial
You are fortunate
You will find happiness

HOROSCOPES

HAVE YOU got a movie star heart throb or a personal pop idol? Or maybe you fancy someone at school? Use this chart to find out if you and he are meant to be!

Just look up your star sign on the left-hand side of the chart, then move along the line until you are under the column where his birthday falls.

Then check out the friendship or love potential. Look up the meaning of the symbols on the key below.

♥ Love
☺ Friendship
☠ Danger
! Caution
? Take a chance

	Aries March 21 – April 19	Taurus April 20 – May 20	Gemini May 21 – June 21	Cancer June 22 – July 22	Leo July 23 – August 22
Aries	?	☺	!	☠	♥
Taurus	!	♥	☠	♥	!
Gemini	♥	☠	?	☠	☺
Cancer	☠	☺	☠	♥	?
Leo	♥	!	♥	☠	☺
Virgo	!	☺	♥	☺	!
Libra	☠	♥	☺	?	♥
Scorpio	♥	?	☠	☠	!
Sagittarius	☺	☠	♥	?	☺
Capricorn	☠	♥	☠	☺	?
Aquarius	☺	☠	☺	!	♥
Pisces	☠	♥	☺	☠	♥

Virgo	Libra	Scorpio	Sagittarius	Capricorn	Aquarius	Pisces
August 23 – September 22	September 23 – October 22	October 23 – November 21	November 22 – December 21	December 22 – January 19	January 20 – February 18	February 19 – March 20
☠	☺	!	♥	☠	☺	?
☺	♥	♥	☠	?	!	☺
!	♥	☺	☺	☠	☺	!
☠	♥	!	☠	♥	☠	♥
?	!	♥	☺	☠	?	☺
☺	?	!	?	♥	☺	?
☠	♥	!	?	☺	☺	♥
☺	☠	?	☺	☺	☠	♥
♥	☺	☠	!	☠	☺	♥
♥	☠	!	☺	♥	☺	!
☠	♥	☠	♥	☺	?	☺
?	☺	♥	☺	?	☺	!

Pajama-rama

Once you are in your pajamas, it's time for a bedtime story. Plump up those pillows and grab a cuddly animal!

Story cards

Sometimes story-telling is easier – and more fun – if you have a starting point. Try this! Write a collection of words and phrases on cards. Put the cards in a box and use them as prompts to help you tell a story.

Each person takes it in turn to be the storyteller, telling a complete story from beginning to end. You could devise your own set of rules, such as the storyteller must use no fewer than five cards and no more than ten, or that she should start with one card and pick another one each time one of the other players rings a bell! Or that she can pick a card every time she starts a new sentence! You decide.

On the right are some ideas for words to write on your cards. Make as many cards as you can, so you don't run out of themes too quickly or have to repeat the themes too often! Find a nice box to keep them in and you can use them for your story-telling on other occasions in the future.

One-word stories

A great way to make up a story is to build it up saying one word each, in turn. It can be difficult to keep going for more than a few minutes, before someone has a fit of the giggles – but it's fun trying!

Sit in a circle and go round clockwise, with each person saying a single word. For example, it might go: **"Once – upon – a – time – in – a – land – far – away – there – lived – a – beautiful – gorgeous – clever – delightful – "** and so on!

Once upon a time
the fairy queen
a handsome prince
Sir Hector Droopy Drawers
King Bobby the Second
Princess Esmerelda
in a suitcase
the tallest tower
under the bed
five purple pixies
a dozen rabbits
a magic sheep
sparkling blue eyes
on a bicycle
a good fairy
the wooden drawbridge
a scarlet cape
a jewel-encrusted crown
pink satin pants
walking in the woods
suddenly disappeared
the spiral staircase
wicked witch
a secret casket
a big warty nose
a magic spell
a broken wand
sound of a horse's hooves
"Will you marry me?"
a sudden earthquake
tied up in knots
an enormous fortune
happily ever after

So, as you take cards out of the box and try to weave the words into your story, it might go something like this...

"**Princess Esmerelda** sat alone in her room at the top of **the tallest tower** in the castle. It was her 21st birthday tomorrow and if she hadn't found **a handsome prince** by lunchtime, her parents would make her marry the hideous **Sir Hector Droopy Drawers**. Just then, she heard the **sound of a horse's hooves** galloping over **the wooden drawbridge**. It was probably only the cook, returning from market with **a dozen rabbits** for dinner. Peeping out of the window she saw that the rider was not the cook but a gorgeous young man in **a scarlet cape** and **pink satin pants**. She couldn't see his face, so she decided to go downstairs to get a better look. But as she descended **the spiral staircase**, she tripped and ..."

Dream team

When you wake up in the morning, try to remember what you dreamed last night. Did you dream you were flying, or swimming, or eating a giant cream cake? And what does it all mean? Tell each other your dreams and have a go at interpreting their meanings with the help of these definitions.

Children A sign of happiness
Doll Stand up for yourself
Angel Expect a messenger
Ghost Someone needs your help
Magician Is someone deceiving you?
Actor or actress Try to be yourself

Clothes Are you putting on an act?
Umbrella You are looking for protection, or feeling abandoned
Bag You need to get away, or put things aside
Jewelry You have lots of hopes and dreams
Hat You wish to change your personality
Gloves You feel secure

Clock Stop wasting time
Prison Do you feel trapped?
School You need to solve a problem
Ladder You're looking for happiness
Exams Are you being too critical of yourself?
Book You will learn more about yourself

Fire Try to keep control of things
Water You feel tranquil, or you need more freedom
Thunder You are angry or afraid
Sun You feel secure and confident
Earthquake You are under a lot of pressure
Volcano You're about to lose your temper

Tower You are ambitious
Castle You want to be dominant
Island You need more time to yourself
House You may need a new challenge
Countryside You are feeling happy and fulfilled
Cave Are you hiding? Do you need to face up to something?

Cat You desire something
Dog You are loyal and devoted
Pig Someone is being selfish or unwise
Lion Are you being too proud or masterful?
Snake Spiritual energy, wisdom, and healing
Rat Have you been disloyal? Or have you got an enemy?

Keepsake book

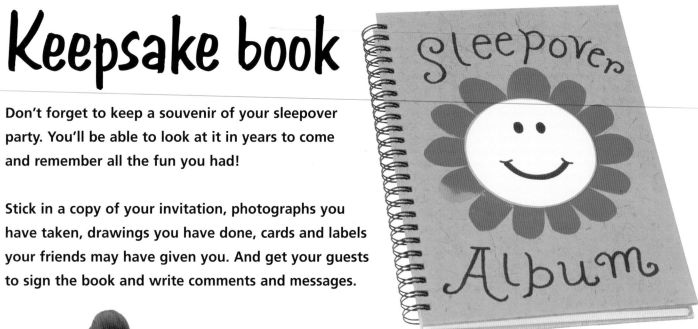

Don't forget to keep a souvenir of your sleepover party. You'll be able to look at it in years to come and remember all the fun you had!

Stick in a copy of your invitation, photographs you have taken, drawings you have done, cards and labels your friends may have given you. And get your guests to sign the book and write comments and messages.

*Capture the **moment**! Take photos of each other in your party outfits, street clothes, dressing-up clothes – whatever! Take it in turns to be the photographer. You could even get a grown-up to help – at least then you'll then get a picture of everyone together!*

When you take a photo try to make sure you have a steady hand or the picture will be blurry!

Taking photographs

There is an art to taking a good photo! To ensure a good result every time (well, almost every time), try these tips:
- pose your subjects against a plain background, with no distracting clutter
- make sure you can see everyone – it's a good idea to put the tallest person at the back or in the middle

- move in close so you're taking a picture of your friends, rather than their surroundings!
- everyone should be relaxed – try telling a joke to make them smile
- take more than one photo, so you have several to choose from

Have fun making up your album

Here are a few items you may find useful:
- choose a suitable book – a spiral-bound notebook is ideal, or maybe a ring binder
- have a pair of scissors handy, to trim photos and other items to size
- use a glue stick to stick things on the pages – easy to use and not too much mess!
- pens and colored pencils are invaluable for adding captions and doodles!
- decorate pages with colorful stickers!

Cameras that produce "instant" pictures are great fun to use.

Things to trace

Aa Bb Cc Dd Ee Ff
Gg Hh Ii Jj Kk Ll
Mm Nn Oo Pp Qq
Rr Ss Tt Uu Vv
Ww Xx Yy Zz

Sleepover Party

use this template to make the
party bunting on page 12